FAMILY Lasts Forever

A VERY SPECIAL BABY BOOK

SHEILA B FRASCHT & NOELLE K ANDREW

FAMILY
Lasts Forever

SHEILA B FRASCHT RN, CHPPN, CPLC
NOELLE K ANDREW MDIV, BCC
ILLUSTRATIONS BY NINA SCOTT

Sometimes love is for a moment.
Sometimes love is for a lifetime.
Sometimes a moment is a lifetime.

Anonymous

Dedication page

This baby book is dedicated to mothers and fathers who have received unexpected news about their unborn baby's health. When facing the fear of the unknown, the loss of dreams, and an uncertain future, they have shown great strength, trust, and the power of love. It is also dedicated to their remarkable babies. Though yet unseen, they teach us profound lessons about strength, grace, and hope.

Lastly, this book is dedicated to our own daughters, Annika and Emily. Their journeys—though different from each other's but both unexpected—have made us mothers who love our daughters fiercely and who strive to always see the blessings in life.

The Family I Dreamed Of and Hoped For

_____

_____

_____

_____

_____

_____

_____

_____

_____

_____

We're Having a Baby!

_____

_____

_____

_____

_____

_____

_____

_____

_____

_____

_____

_____

_____

_____

_____

_____

_____

_____

_____

"A great joy is coming."
Author Unknown

When I Think of You...

"She will bring light, love, peace, and joy as her gifts to this world."

Kim Fehlhafer, grandmother of Cecilia

Hearing the News that Changed Our Lives Forever

_____

_____

_____

_____

_____

_____

_____

_____

_____

"It was the moment they sat me up and said there were major complications with our baby that my world seemed to turn upside-down."

Annette Miller, mother of Kaitlyn

"How do you tell your parents that their grandson might not survive? There were times when we felt angry. There were times when we questioned, "Why us?" There were moments of jealousy, seeing pictures and posts from people having healthy babies."

David Anderson, father of Matthew

Getting to Know You in a New Light

_____

_____

_____

_____

_____

_____

_____

_____

_____

_____

"Because of Matthew, I know what it means to recognize the important things in life."

Michelle Anderson, mother of Matthew

The Savannah I See

Dedicated to Savannah Houselog

Written by Beth Houselog, her mother, on 8/13/2013
Savannah was born on 9/23/13

In you, they see minutes.
In you, I see eternity.

In you, they see birth defects.
In you, I see possibilities and perfection.

In you, they see a fetus.
In you, I see my sweet darling baby daughter.

In you, they see lots of hold-ups.
In you, I see "Why not?" and "What if you tried this?"

In you, they see life's end.
In you, I see my future.

In you, they see "quality vs. quantity."
In you, I cannot separate the two. I want you here on Earth with us.

In you, they see no miracles.
In you, I see one of the greatest miracles--
You have made it so far and I am so proud of you.

In you, they see a life.
In you, I see the most important life.

You are loved beyond measure and wanted beyond compare.

Continuing On, Day By Day

_____

_____

_____

_____

_____

_____

_____

_____

_____

"When I found out my child was sick, my world just stopped. I lost myself in the time I had with him. I didn't know how long that would be, but every kick, every hiccup was the greatest feeling in the world."

Michelle Anderson, mother of Matthew

Times When It Is the Hardest

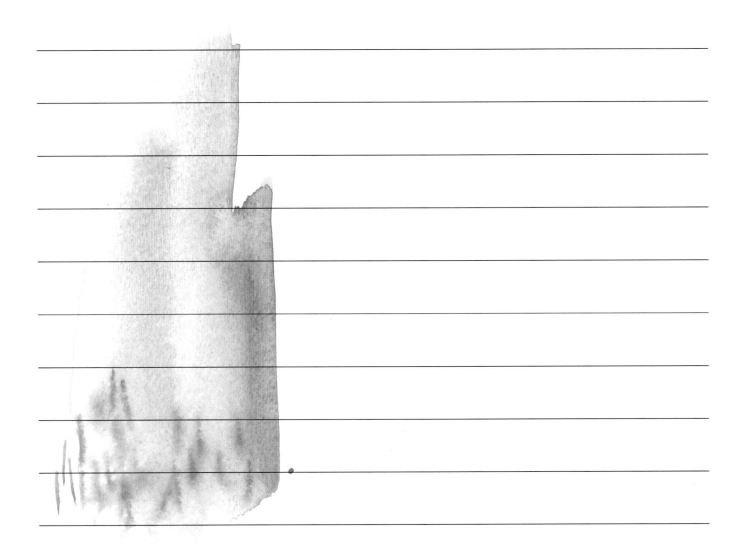

"The rain outside matches my mood. I feel like creation is crying with me at the unfairness of this whole situation."

Annette Miller, mother of Kaitlyn

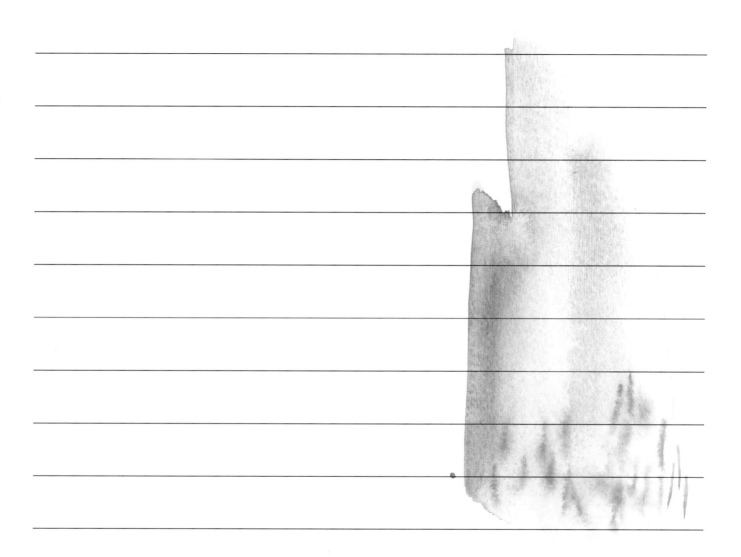

"The truth is I feel like there is not language for the grief or complexity of all the emotions of losing a child. If there is, I lack the vocabulary."

Ledru Miller, father of Kaitlyn

Reclaiming Joy and Anticipation

_____

_____

_____

_____

_____

_____

_____

_____

_____

"I love feeling you move. Each kick and flutter is like you're having a conversation with me. I want to always remember how this feels!"

Annette Miller, mother of Kaitlyn

Wearisome Emotions

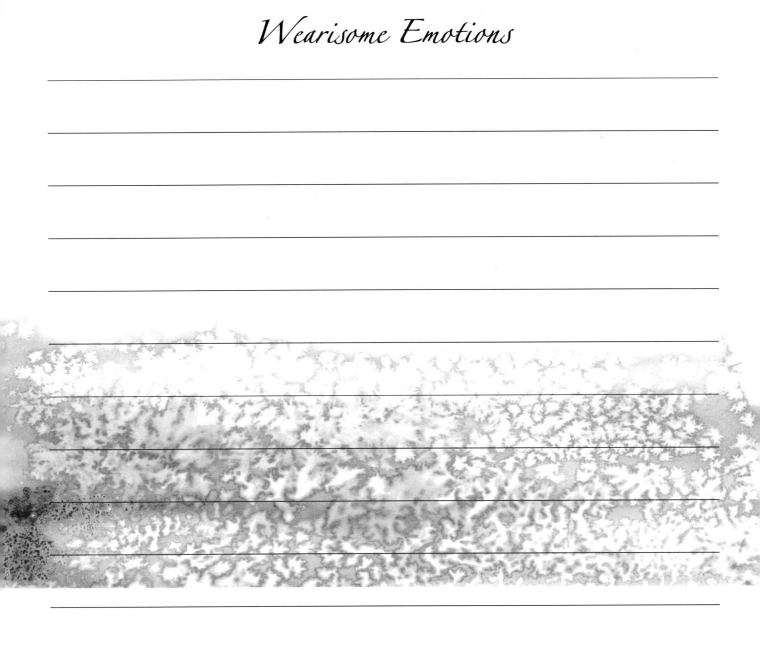

"We always prayed that it would turn out for the best."

Gary and Dee Anderson, grandparents of Matthew

Things That Make It a Bit "Easier"

_____

_____

_____

_____

_____

_____

_____

_____

_____

_____

_____

_____

_____

_____

_____

_____

_____

_____

_____

"I am so grateful that we asked for support. We trusted our doctors, nurses and support team to guide us with Cecilia's highest good as our only goal."

Kim Fehlhafer, grandmother of Cecilia

Ways You Let Us Know You Are Here

As Matthew's mommy, I feel blessed. I was able to bond with him like no one else could. He was part of me and I knew his personality. He was protective and by not letting the doctors see what they needed...he gave us hope."

Michelle Anderson, mother of Matthew

What I Look Forward To

_____

_____

_____

_____

_____

_____

_____

_____

_____

_____

_____

"Finding out about your medical problems seemed almost impossible to comprehend. We were totally unprepared to let go of our dreams of who we thought you would be. What we came to realize, though, is that you were exactly who you were meant to be and we couldn't wait to find out what blessings you would bring to our family."

Sheila Frascht, mother of Annika

Getting Ready to Meet You

_____

_____

_____

_____

_____

_____

_____

_____

_____

"When I look back at how everything happened, I wouldn't change a thing."

David Anderson, father of Matthew

Your Birth Day

_____

_____

_____

_____

_____

_____

_____

_____

_____

"Today we celebrate what was given to us, not what was taken away."

Mark McKinley, father of Cecilia

How You've Changed Us

"The whole experience leading up to the time of Matthew's birth brought the two families closer together and showed us that with faith in God and the love of family, we can get through anything."

Mike and Deb Hatting, grandparents of Matthew

You Have Made Your Mark on This World

_____

_____

_____

_____

_____

_____

_____

_____

"We try on a daily basis to go out of our way to make someone else's day a little better. Sometimes it's opening a door for someone, reaching out to an old friend or donating to a charity. We call it 'doing our Matthews'."

David Anderson, father of Matthew

"We began to accept that Cecilia's life may not have been intended to be a long life. We also realized that it made her mission of love no less valuable. I see the evidence of her life and the love she inspired still rippling through my life and the lives of those she touched."

Kim Fehlhafer, grandmother of Cecilia

Also available from these authors:

"Love Lasts Forever:
A Journal of Memories"